Introduction

The potato is a vegetable of great versatility. It can be baked, roasted, fried, boiled, mashed, puréed and chipped. Potatoes make great hot and cold salads as well as wholesome accompaniments to main meals.

Choice of potato is important. For mashing or baking in jackets, buy potatoes with a light and floury texture such as Maris Piper or Cara. If you want potatoes which hold their shape, opt for firm varieties with a close texture when cooked such as Desirée or new potatoes. Look before you buy is a sound tip and either seek your greengrocer's advice, or check descriptions given by supermarkets which usually tell you the name and characteristics of a particular type.

... =

... not

Eggs used are a medium size [illegible]er-wise stated.

For additional hints and tips on preparing potatoes, see step-by-step instructions and pictures on pages 18-19 and 34-35.

Kilojoules and kilocalories at the end of each recipe are represented by the letters kJ and kcal.

Designed by Clive Dorman & Co.
Printed in Italy by G. Canale & C.S.p.A

Distributed in the UK by J.B. Fairfax Press Limited, 9 Trinity Centre, Park Farm, Wellingborough, Northants NN8 6ZB

Distributed in Australia by J.B. Fairfax Press Pty Ltd, 80 McLachlan Avenue, Rushcutters Bay, Sydney, NSW 2011

Written by Annette Wolter

Potato Gnocchi

Serves 4

A speciality of Italy, these tasty dumplings are made from potatoes and cheese.

Preparation time: about 40 minutes
Cooking time: 45 minutes

1kg (2lb) floury potatoes
12 slightly heaped tablespoons plain flour
1 teaspoon salt
3 egg yolks
¼ teaspoon freshly milled white pepper
½ teaspoon dried marjoram
About 3 litres (5¼ pints/12 cups) water
2 teaspoons salt
75g (2½ oz) grated Parmesan cheese
45g (1½ oz) butter or margarine
1 tablespoon chopped parsley
Onion rings, black olives, lettuce and tomato slices for garnishing, optional

1 Peel and wash potatoes. Cut into chunks and cook in boiling salted water until soft. Drain off water. Mash in saucepan with potato masher or large fork. Cool slightly.

2 Mix in flour, 1teaspoon salt, egg yolks, pepper and marjoram.

3 To cook gnocchi, bring water to boil in large saucepan. Add salt. Preheat oven to 200C (400F/Gas 6). Grease a 25cm (10in) fluted flan dish with a little butter or margarine.

4 Using 2 wetted tablespoons, shape potato mixture into ovals and slide into gently simmering water. Cook, uncovered, until gnocchi float to surface. Lift out of pan with draining spoon. Transfer to plate lined with absorbent kitchen paper.

5 Transfer gnocchi to prepared dish and sprinkle with cheese. Top with flakes of butter or margarine and scatter chopped parsley over. Bake in oven for 10-15 minutes until top is golden brown. Garnish, if liked and serve hot.

Nutritional value per portion:
about 1700kj/400kcal
Protein: 15g
Fat: 18g
Carbohydrate: 46g

Potato Gnocchi

Swiss Rosti

Serves 4

A wonderful potato pancake from Switzerland.

Preparation time: about 30 minutes
Cooking time: 1 hour 20 minutes

750g (1½ lb) firm potatoes, peeled and boiled the previous day
125g (4oz) streaky bacon, rind removed
2 medium onions
3 tablespoons sunflower or corn oil
½ teaspoon salt
¼ teaspoon freshly milled black pepper
Chopped fresh parsley and grilled bacon rashers for garnishing

1 Grate potatoes coarsely into mixing bowl.

2 Coarsely chop bacon. Peel and finely chop onions. Heat oil in large frying pan and sauté bacon and onions until light golden brown, stirring frequently. Stir in grated potatoes, salt and pepper then divide mixture into 4 portions. Preheat oven to 110C (225F/Gas¼).

3 Put one portion of potato mixture into 15cm (6in) heavy-based and lightly greased non-stick frying pan and flatten with back of spoon until base of pan is covered.

4 Fry potatoes until underside is crisp and golden brown and rosti is holding together. Turn over with large fish slice and fry second side until golden brown. Transfer rosti to large heatproof plate lined with absorbent kitchen paper and keep warm in oven.

5 Repeat process to make 3 more pancakes. Serve hot rosti garnished with parsley and bacon. If liked, top with a generous sprinkling of grated Gruyère cheese and accompany with salad.

TIPS

1 For a complete meal, serve with a large mixed salad tossed with French dressing.
2 Instead of turning pancakes over with fish slice, try this technique: Put saucepan lid over frying pan and holding lid in place with one hand, invert pan so pancake lies on top of saucepan lid, cooked side facing uppermost. Gently slide pancake back into pan and cook second side until golden brown. Transfer to large heatproof plate lined with absorbent kitchen paper and keep warm in oven.

Nutritional value per portion:
about 1700kj/400kcal
Protein: 7g
Fat: 28g
Carbohydrate: 35g

Swiss Rosti

Potato Pancakes with Syrup

Serves 4

Marvellous for winter teas and an interesting change from traditional crumpets or muffins.

Preparation time: about 50 minutes
Cooking time: about 30 minutes

750g (1½ lb) floury potatoes
2 medium eggs, beaten
4 tablespoons plain flour
1 teaspoon salt
3 tablespoon sunflower or corn oil
Maple syrup or golden syrup for serving

1 Peel and wash potatoes and grate directly into mixing bowl. Stir in eggs, flour and salt. Preheat oven to 110C (225F/Gas¼).

2 Heat one third of oil in 25cm (10in) non-stick frying pan until hot. Using table-spoon, add 4 large spoonfuls of potato mixture to pan and flatten into rounds with back of spoon.

3 Fry pancakes for 3 minutes. Turn over with spatula and fry for a further 3 minutes until crisp and golden. Drain on absorbent kitchen paper. Transfer pancakes to baking tray and keep warm in oven.

4 Repeat process, using up remaining oil and potato mixture. Serve pancakes warm with warm syrup.

Nutritional value per portion:
about 3000kj/710kcal
Protein: 12g
Fat: 23g
Carbohydrate: 120g

Potato Pancakes with Syrup

Golden Potato Salad

Serves 4

A colourful salad which makes a good accompaniment to grilled fish, meat and poultry.

Preparation time: about 30 minutes
Standing time: 2 hours

1Kg (2lb) firm potatoes or new potatoes, peeled and cooked the day before
2 medium onions
280ml (9fl oz/1 cup) vegetable stock
3 tablespoons tarragon vinegar
1 teaspoon salt
¼ teaspoon freshly milled pepper
2 medium tomatoes
3 large hard-boiled eggs
4 tablespoons sunflower or corn oil
2 tablespoons snipped fresh chives

1 Slice potatoes fairly thinly. Finely chop onions. Put both into large mixing bowl.

2 Bring stock to boil and pour over potatoes and onions. Add vinegar and season with salt and pepper. Mix thoroughly, cover and leave to stand at room temperature for 2 hours.

3 Meanwhile, cover tomatoes with boiling water for 30 seconds, then plunge into cold water and peel away skins. Cut tomatoes in half, discard any pieces of hard core and chop flesh.

4 Shell eggs, thinly slice and set aside.

5 Stir potato and onion mixture and adjust seasoning to taste. Trickle oil over top then gently toss potato mixture until thoroughly mixed.

6 Spoon potato and onion mixture into centre of large serving dish and arrange egg slices round edges. Sprinkle salad with chives and serve.

Nutritional value per portion:
about1400kj/330kcal
Protein: 10g
Fat: 12g
Carbohydrate: 46g

Golden Potato Salad

Swedish Potato Salad

Serves 4

A piquant and typically Swedish salad made from rollmops, new potatoes and beetroot.

Preparation time: about 45 minutes
Standing time: 2 hours

750g (1½ lb) new potatoes
3 hard-boiled eggs
1 large onion
2 pickled cucumbers
1 large eating apple
2 rollmop herrings, drained
220g (7oz) cooked beetroot
Salt and pepper to taste
2 teaspoons mild Continental mustard
2 tablespoons white wine vinegar
4 tablespoons sunflower or corn oil
2 teaspoons tomato purée (paste)
Chopped fresh dill for garnishing

1 Scrape potatoes clean under cold running water. Cook in boiling salted water until tender, keeping pan two-thirds covered. Drain potatoes and cool.

2 Shell eggs and halve. Remove yolks and set aside. Coarsely chop egg whites.

3 Peel and finely chop onion and pickled cucumbers. Peel, quarter and core apple, then cut into small pieces.

4 Halve rollmops lengthwise and cut flesh into 1cm (½ in) pieces. Peel beetroot, thinly slice and cut into thin strips.

5 Dice potatoes and put into mixing bowl. Add prepared ingredients and season with salt and pepper. Arrange on large plate.

6 Rub egg yolks through fine sieve into small bowl. Beat in mustard, vinegar, oil and tomato purée (paste). Scatter with fresh chopped dill.

7 Spoon egg yolk dressing over centre of salad and garnish with fresh dill seed head, if liked.

Nutritional value per portion:
about 1700kj/400kcal
Protein: 15g
Fat: 23g
Carbohydrate: 37g

Swedish Potato Salad

Farmer's Breakfast

Serves 4

A fried potato, bacon, egg and onion dish perfect for a leisurely weekend breakfast.

Preparation time: about 30 minutes
Cooking time: about 30 minutes

1Kg (2lb) firm potatoes, peeled and boiled the previous day
220g (7oz) streaky bacon, rind removed
1 large onion
15g (½ oz) butter
1 teaspoon salt
¼ teaspoon pepper
4 eggs
1 tablespoon chopped fresh parsley for garnishing
1 tablespoon chopped fresh chives for garnishing

1 Thinly slice potatoes. Finely chop bacon. Peel onion and chop finely.

2 Melt butter in large heavy-based frying pan until hot. Add bacon and onion and sauté over moderate heat until light golden.

3 Mix in potatoes, season with salt and pepper and sauté until golden brown, stirring frequently.

4 Beat eggs until frothy. Pour into pan, lifting up potato mixture round edges to enable eggs to flow into gaps.

5 Continue to fry until eggs are just set. Sprinkle with parsley and chives, spoon on to 4 warm serving plates and serve straight away.

Nutritional value per portion:
about 230kj/550kcal
Protein: 17g
Fat: 25g
Carbohydrate: 63g

Farmer's Breakfast

Potato and Minced Beef Casserole

Serves 4

Handy for a mid-week meal with cooked green vegetables.

Preparation time: about 50 minutes
Cooking time: 25 minutes

750g (1½ lb) floury potatoes
2 medium red peppers (capsicum)
2 medium onions
3 tablespoons sunflower or corn oil
410g (14oz) lean minced beef
4 tablespoons fresh white or brown breadcrumbs
2 eggs, beaten
1½ teaspoons salt
2 teaspoons paprika
60g (2oz) Caerphilly or Wensleydale cheese
155ml (5fl oz/⅔ cup) thick sour cream
2 tablespoons chopped fresh parsley
Sprig of fresh parsley for garnishing

1 Peel potatoes and cook in boiling salted water until tender. Drain, cool and slice.

2 Halve peppers (capsicum), remove inner white membranes and seeds then cut flesh into narrow strips. Peel onions and finely slice.

3 Heat half the oil in saucepan. Add onions and sauté fairly slowly until transparent and just beginning to soften. Mix in pepper (capsicum) strips and stir-fry for 5 minutes.

4 In separate pan, heat remaining oil until hot, but not smoking. Add beef and stir-fry briskly until well-browned and crumbly. Mix in 2 tablespoons of the breadcrumbs, eggs, salt and paprika. Stir well.

5 Preheat oven to 220C (425F/Gas 7). Grease a heatproof casserole dish with margarine. Fill with alternate layers of potatoes, sautéed onions and peppers (capsicums) and beef mixture, ending with a layer of potatoes. Sprinkle top with remaining breadcrumbs

6 Grate or crumble cheese, mix with sour cream and parsley then spoon over top of casserole.

7 Bake in oven for 25 minutes until golden brown. Garnish with parsley sprig and serve.

Nutritional value per portion:
about 2500kj/600kcal
Protein: 34g
Fat: 34g
Carbohydrate: 37g

Potato and Minced Beef Casserole

Step-by step

Boiling Potatoes in the Skins

1 Scrub potatoes clean under cold running water.

2 Put into saucepan and add water to just cover. Stir in salt and cover with lid.

3 Cook potatoes for 25-35 minutes or until tender. Drain and use as required.

How to Sauté Potatoes

4 Cut cooked and peeled potatoes into large cubes. Finely chop onion and bacon.

5 Heat oil or margarine in large heavy-based frying pan. Add onion and bacon and sauté until golden brown. Add potato and sauté until golden, stirring frequently.

6 For sliced sauté potatoes, cut cooked potatoes into medium thick slices. Heat oil, margarine or clarified (concentrated) butter in heavy-based pan. A non-stick pan is best. Sauté over moderate heat until potatoes are golden brown, turning frequently.

Jacket Potatoes in Foil

7 Scrub potatoes clean under cold running water and wipe dry. Prick each potato in 6 places with fork. Wrap securely in foil and put directly onto oven rack.

8 Bake in preheated oven set to 220C (425F/Gas 7) for about 1 hour or until tender when pierced with a skewer.

9 Leave potatoes to stand for about 5 minutes then carefully unwrap and cut a cross on top of each. Press with tea towel until cuts open up. Serve with butter, grated cheese, sour cream or sauce.

1

4

7

2

3

5

6

8

9

Hot Potatoes with Cold Cheese Sauce

Serves 4

New potatoes topped with a creamy Stilton cheese sauce.

Preparation time: about 40 minutes

1Kg (2lb) small new potatoes
250g (8oz) fromage frais or skimmed milk soft cheese
155g (5oz) Stilton cheese
5 tablespoons crème fraîche
Pinch of cayenne pepper
Salt to taste
2 tablespoons snipped fresh chives

1 Scrape potatoes clean under cold running water. Cook in boiling salted water until tender and drain. Return potatoes to pan and cover with a clean tea towel so they keep hot.

2 For sauce, spoon fromage frais or soft cheese into mixing bowl. Crumble in Stilton cheese then stir in crème fraîche, cayenne pepper and chives.

3 Transfer potatoes to a warm dish, coat with sauce and serve straight away. Dust top with extra cayenne or paprika pepper and more snipped fresh chives, if liked.

Nutritional value per portion:
about 2500kj/600kcal
Protein: 34g
Fat: 34g
Carbohydrate: 37g

Hot Potatoes with Cold Cheese Sauce

Gratin Dauphinoise

Serves 4

A versatile dish of potatoes, Gruyère cheese and cream, perfect to serve with all grilled meats and fish.

Preparation time: about 40 minutes
Cooking time: 50 minutes

1Kg (2lb) floury potatoes
1 clove garlic
125g (4oz) Gruyère cheese
410ml (13fl oz/1⅔ cups) milk
1 teaspoon salt
White pepper to taste
About 30g (1oz) butter or margarine
2 eggs
4 tablespoons whipping cream
Sprig of fresh parsley and 1 tablespoon chopped for garnishing

1 Peel potatoes and wipe dry with absorbent kitchen paper. Cut into wafer-thin slices.

2 Peel garlic and crush on to plate. Grate cheese. Preheat oven to 220C (425F/Gas 7).

3 Bring milk to boil and season to taste with salt and pepper. Using some of the butter or margarine, well-grease a large oval gratin dish. Sprinkle base with garlic.

4 Fill dish with half the potato slices, half the cheese and remaining potatoes. Pour over hot milk. Bake gratin in oven for 40 minutes, then remove.

5 Beat eggs with cream and pour over gratin. Sprinkle with remaining cheese and dot with flakes of butter or margarine.

6 Return potatoes to oven and continue to bake for a further 10 minutes. Garnish with parsley and serve.

Nutritional value per portion:
about 1800kj/430kcal
Protein: 19g
Fat: 18g
Carbohydrate: 45g

Gratin Dauphinoise

Potato Tortilla

Serves 4

This version of the classic Spanish tortilla has a slight Mexican influence.

Preparation time: about 1 hour

750g (1½ lb) floury potatoes
1 large onion
2 green peppers (capsicums)
2 beef tomatoes
3 tablespoons sunflower or corn oil
4 eggs
1teaspoon salt
3 drops Tabasco sauce
220g (7oz) canned sweetcorn, drained
Chopped fresh parsley for garnishing

1 Peel potatoes, wipe dry then thinly slice.

2 Peel onion and thinly slice. Separate onion into rings. Halve peppers (capsicums) and remove inner white membranes and seeds. Cut flesh into 1cm (½ in) wide strips. Cover tomatoes with boiling water for 30 seconds, then plunge into cold water and peel away skins. Cut tomatoes in half, discard any pieces of hard core and slice flesh.

3 Heat oil in a large heavy-based, non-stick frying pan. Add onions and sauté gently until transparent and just beginning to soften.

4 Add potato slices and pepper (capsicum) strips. Mix in well and sauté fairly gently for 10 minutes or until potatoes are tender, stirring frequently. Add tomato.

5 Beat eggs with salt and Tabasco until foamy and pour over sautéed vegetable mixture.

6 Sprinkle with sweetcorn. Partially cover pan with lid and cook gently for 7 minutes. Sprinkle with chopped fresh parsley, cut tortilla into portions and serve with French bread.

Nutritional value per portion:
about 2100kj/500kcal
Protein: 15g
Fat: 26g
Carbohydrate: 51g

Potato Tortilla

Caraway Potatoes with Cheese Topping

Serves 4

An unusual treatment for jacket potatoes. If preferred, use sesame seeds instead of caraway.

Preparation time: about 20 minutes
Baking time: 35 minutes

8 medium elongated-shaped floury potatoes
4 tablespoons sunflower or corn oil
salt and pepper to taste
3 teaspoons caraway or sesame seeds
Sprigs of fresh basil and rosemary for garnishing

CHEESE TOPPING
2 medium onions
4 tablespoons snipped fresh chives
2 sprigs each of fresh basil, dill and rosemary, chopped
500g (1lb) fromage frais or skimmed milk soft cheese
Salt and freshly milled pepper
5 tablespoons single cream

1 Preheat oven to 200C (400F/Gas 6). Line a shallow baking tin with foil, shiny-side facing uppermost, and brush lightly with oil.

2 Scrub potatoes clean under cold running water and pat dry with absorbent kitchen paper. Halve each potato lengthwise.

3 Brush cut sides of potato halves liberally with oil. Sprinkle with salt and caraway seeds. Arrange potatoes, cut-sides down, on prepared tray and bake in oven for 35 minutes.

4 Meanwhile, peel onions and finely chop or grate. Put into mixing bowl and add chives, basil, dill and rosemary.

5 Mix in fromage frais or soft cheese, salt, pepper and cream. Beat lightly until smooth, serve with baked potatoes and garnish with herb sprigs.

Nutritional value per portion:
about 2200kj/520kcal
Protein: 23g
Fat: 25g
Carbohydrate: 49g

Caraway Potatoes with Cheese Topping

Potato Purée with Garlic and Walnuts

Serves 4

Eaten with courgettes (zucchini) and tomatoes, this Grecian main course is a perfect choice for vegetarians,

Preparation time: about 1¼ hours

750g (1½ lb) floury potatoes
750g (1½ lb) courgettes (zucchini)
8 tablespoons plain flour
2 teaspoons salt
Pepper to taste
4 tablespoons olive oil
5 cloves garlic, crushed
60g (2oz) chopped walnut halves
2 teaspoons white wine vinegar
Tomato slices and fresh parsley for garnishing

1 Peel potatoes and cut into chunks. Cook in boiling salted water for about 25-30 minutes or until tender.

2 Meanwhile, top and tail courgettes (zucchini) and cut each lengthwise into 1cm (1/2 in) thick slices. Preheat oven to 110C (225F/Gas¼).

3 Mix flour, half the salt and pepper to taste in a shallow dish. Add courgette (zucchini) slices, one at a time, and coat on both sides with flour mixture.

4 Heat half the oil in heavy-based, non-stick frying pan. Add courgette (zucchini) slices, a few at a time, and fry briskly until crisp and golden on both sides, turning twice. Drain on heatproof plate lined with absorbent kitchen paper and keep warm in oven.

5 Drain potatoes and return to saucepan. Mash finely and beat in remaining oil and salt. Season with pepper to taste. Mix in garlic, nuts and vinegar.

6 Reheat potatoes until piping hot, stirring occasionally. Serve straight away with courgettes (zucchini) and garnish with tomatoes and parsley.

Nutritional value per person:
about 2900kj/690kcal
Protein: 11g
Fat: 47g
Carbohydrate: 56g

Potato Purée with Garlic and Walnuts

Jacket Potatoes with Sour Cream Dressing

Serves 4

A modern classic to serve with poultry, meat dishes and burgers.

Preparation time: about 20 minutes
Cooking time: 1 hour 15 minutes

4 medium floury potatoes

DRESSING

3 tablespoons each fresh dill, chervil, parsley and chives
315ml (10fl oz/1¼ cups) thick fresh soured cream
Salt and pepper to taste

1 Preheat oven to 220C (425F/Gas 7). Prepare jacket potatoes for baking in foil following instructions and step-by-step pictures on pages 18-19.

2 To make cream dressing, wash herbs, wipe dry with absorbent kitchen paper and finely chop.

3 Tip cream into bowl. Stir in prepared herbs and season to taste with salt and pepper.

4 Unwrap potatoes. Cut a cross on top of each then squeeze open with help of folded tea towel.

5 Put potatoes on to 4 warm serving plates, add plenty of dressing to each and serve straight away with chosen main course.

TIPS

1 A few teaspoons of chopped salted peanuts can be added with herbs.
2 Substitute chopped watercress for the herbs listed in the recipe.

Nutritional value per portion:
about 1100kj/260kcal
Protein: 7g
Fat: 6g
Carbohydrate: 43g

Jacket Potatoes with Sour Cream Dressing

Potatoes with Gammon and Mushrooms

Serves 4

Ring the changes with this aniseed-flavoured potato and gammon casserole.

Preparation time: 1 hour

750g (1½ lb) firm potatoes
3 shallots
500g (1lb) mushrooms
185g (6oz) gammon
60g (2oz) margarine
280ml (9 fl oz/1 cup) chicken stock
½ teaspoon herb salt
2 tablespoons snipped fresh chives
2 teaspoons cornflour
1 tablespoon cold water
125g (4oz) crème fraîche
¼ teaspoon fennel seeds

1 Peel potatoes and halve or quarter depending on size. Cook in boiling salted water until tender. Drain, peel and slice.

2 Peel and finely chop shallots. Trim mushrooms, wipe clean and slice thinly. Cut gammon into thin strips.

3 Melt margarine in heavy-based saucepan. Add shallots and sauté until transparent and just beginning to soften. Add gammon and mushrooms and stir-fry for 2 minutes.

4 Bring stock to the boil and pour over sautéed vegetables and gammon. Stir in potatoes, herb salt and half the chives.

5 Mix cornflour with cold water until smooth. Add to potato mixture and bring slowly to the boil, stirring. Gradually blend in crème fraîche.

6 Spoon casserole into warm serving dish and sprinkle with remaining chives and the fennel seeds.

TIP
If preferred, replace fennel seeds with the same amount of toasted sesame seeds.

Nutritional value per portion:
about 2000kj/489kcal
Protein: 25g
Fat: 29g
Carbohydrate: 40g

Potatoes with Gammon and Mushrooms

Step-by step

Creamed Potatoes

1kg (2lb) floury potatoes
1½ teaspoon salt
315ml (10fl oz/1¼ cups) water
220ml (7fl oz/1 cup) milk
¼ teaspoon freshly grated nutmeg
60g (2oz) butter or margarine

1 Scrub clean under cold running water. Wipe dry with absorbent kitchen paper.

1

2 Peel potatoes and remove any blemishes.

3 Cut into medium-sized chunks. Put into saucepan. Add salt and water.

4 Bring to the boil. Lower heat, cover and simmer for 25 minutes until potatoes are soft when prodded with a knife.

4

5 Carefully drain off water, holding pan handles and lid with folded tea towel.

6 Mash potatoes finely with potato masher. Bring milk to the boil. Season with nutmeg.

7 Using strong whisk, beat milk into mashed potato, keeping pan over very low heat.

7

8 Gradually add butter or margarine and continue to stir with whisk until mixture is smooth and creamy.

9 Spoon potato into warm serving dish and serve as an accompaniment to main course meals. Garnishes such as fried onion rings, snipped chives mixed with chopped parsley and butter-fried fresh breadcrumbs make interesting toppings.

2

3

5

6

8

9

- Delicious classic and original ideas
- Simple step-by-step instructions
- Every recipe photographed in full colour
- Double-tested by experienced home economists

ISBN 1-874567-41-7

9 781874 567417 >

A JB Fairfax Press Publication